Anne Jung Holden

In Search Of

A Warm Room

A Story of Survival during WW II
As Documented in a Diary

Anne Jung Holden

Warren Publishing

In Search of a Warm Room

Published by:

Warren Publishing

19809 North Cove Road

Cornelius, North Carolina

ISBN 1-886057-83-4

Library of Congress Catalog Number 97-062243

Printed in the United States of America

Dedication

I would like to dedicate this book in memory of my parents, Henry and Katy Jung for their love and devotion.

I would also like to dedicate this book to my husband Ronald L. Holden for his love, encouragement, and support.

About the Author

Anne holds a Bachelor of Science from Ohio University and a Masters in Education from Ashland University. She has taught German at both the high school and college levels for the past twenty-one years.

Anne and her husband Ronald enjoy getting together with their three married children who all live in different parts of the country. They are proud that all of their children are University graduates. They have been blessed with six grandchildren, ages one to nine. They split their time between homes in the Lake Norman area of North Carolina and Mansfield, Ohio.

She enjoys growing flowers as food for the soul, decorating their homes for the tranquility of their daily lives, and baking for the joy of gathering with family and friends.

Having been a Lutheran all her life, she and Ronald are still members of their hometown church, Holy Trinity, in Mansfield Ohio and St. Mark Lutheran Church in Mooresville. NC.

Forward   vi

Chapter I   p.1
A brief history of the Donauschwaben

Chapter II   p.15
The evacuation

Chapter III   p.23
Our journey through Hungary and Austria

Chapter IV   p.35
Our flight to Germany

Chapter V   p.43
The end of World War II

Chapter VI   p.51
Our homeward journey to Crvenka, Yugoslavia

Chapter VII   p.59
Kaisersteinbruck, a barbed wired refugee camp in Austria

Chapter VIII   p.67
The Soviet Zone of Germany

Chapter IX   p.79
Munich, Germany

Chapter X   p.97
Our journey to America

Epilogue   p.111

Batschka Song   p.117

Forward

The end of the first World War began not only the entry of America as a role player in world politics but also the expulsion of people for ethnic reasons. These were humble when compared with what happened at the end of and after World War II. In general it can be said that the victims were almost all German nationals or of German ethnicity living mostly in Eastern Europe. All in all about 20 million persons were targeted and when in 1947 this operation was ended, more than 2.4 million civilian Germans had lost their lives.

Anne Holden tells an unforgettable story of her family's life as ethnic Germans in pre-WWII Yugoslavia and their subsequent expulsion from their homeland by the Communists. Based on the sparse and uncritical diary entries made by her mother during their flight, the author's recollections as a 7-year-old describe what was experienced by thousands of other ethnic Germans who were driven off their land. Anne, to be sure, was lucky since she, with some family members, stayed ahead of the invading Russians and Tito's guerrillas, and thus escaped rape and murder.

When reading this book one has to keep in mind, that with the exception of a handful of relatively small and isolated countries all of Europe was at war. On top of its own "soldatesque" there were combatants from every continent. Mrs. Holden's account, though peripheral, shows that it was nearly impossible for anybody living in the center of Europe, not to be pulled into the fangs of that immensely brutal war. Yet she writes without bitterness and has simply put down a minute piece of history, which should not be forgotten or swept under the rug of ignorance.

Erich-Oskar Wruck, Ph. D. Professor Emeritus
Davidson College

ur people were ethnic Germans who toiled and lived in Austria-Hungary, later called Yugoslavia, for over one hundred fifty years. Toward the end of World War II, the Tito Communists forced us from our homes and lands.

My mother kept a diary from the day we were forced from our home until we found a home again in Munich, Germany, almost two years later. The words in script I have translated directly from my mother's diary. I believe she simply wanted to document this entire experience. She left out her emotions, but recorded only the facts of this event. She wrote her story into a small notebook, which became very tattered toward the end of our journey. Sitting in a corner, she always found a few minutes here and there to document our travels.

I was six years old, almost seven, when we had to leave our town. I remember most of these events distinctly, not in an intellectual way but in the way any six year old remembers events, through the five senses; the way things looked, felt, smelled, tasted, and sounded.

Later on my mother and I would talk about these events. A few days before she died in 1988, she remarked, "Who would have ever imagined that after all those horrible experiences, life could become good again?"

Although the plight of the Jewish people has been well documented, many thousands of ethnic Germans all over Europe had similar experiences. The purpose of this journal is to show what happened to a group of people in the turbulent times of World War II. They were industrious, good people who were caught up in a war that they neither wished for nor could have imagined.

Anne Jung Holden

Chapter I

A brief history of the Donauschwaben

$\mathcal{T}$he Donauschwaben is a group of ethnic Germans who immigrated to a part of the Austrian Empire in the latter part of the 18th Century, which came to be known as Yugoslavia after WWI. Crvenka (Tscherwenka), the town where I was born, is located in the Batschka, a state in Yugoslavia. It is found between the rivers Danube and Theiss – or between Budapest and Belgrade. The two other predominately German settlements were in Romania and Banat.

Sparsely populated and destroyed by the many wars between the Holy Roman Empire and Turkey, the Empress Maria Theresia (1740-1780) began to settle this area with Catholic Germans from the South of Germany (1746). Her son Joseph II (1780-1790) vigorously continued this venture. He believed a source of obtaining a higher standard of living for his subjects could come from the discipline and hard work of farmers and craftsmen. In 1771, on a trip to Paris, he met such people in the Rhineland-Palatinate (Rheinland-Pfalz) area. Perhaps from this experience, he encouraged people from Franconia, Wurttemberg, Hesse, Baden,

Alsace-Lorraine and Rhineland-Palatinate (Rheinland-Pfalz) to settle this territory. The monarch organized and orchestrated this venture well. He arranged for the pioneers to receive the following:

1. Freedom of religion. Clergy and teachers to take care of the needs of the people.

2. A house and garden for each family. Livestock and tools as needed to farm the land.

3. Land and meadows for vineyards.

4. Tools for the craftsmen.

5. Exemption from military service for every first-born son in the family.

6. Free transportation from Vienna and money for the trip on the Danube.

7. Hospitals available for the new emigrants.

8. Exemption from taxation for ten years.

Although the promises must have sounded great, the pioneers were not without hardships. Wars, overpopulation, and a shortage of farmland in their homeland in Germany made people eager to settle this newly available land. They turned a swampy wilderness into fields of grain and bountiful vineyards. Crvenka, because of its central location, became one of the larger settlements in the Batschka.

In 1785, 351 farmers and 164 craftsmen made this town their home. These early settlers had to deal with a humid climate and swampy land. Consequently natural catastrophes such as flooding and illnesses dealt great setbacks to these emigrants. Many died in the early years. They had a saying:

Die ersten fanden den Tod.   The first (settlers) found death.

Die zweiten die Not.   The second misery.

Die dritten das Brot.   The third found bread.

My ancestor, Michael Johann Jung (1760-1823) from Frankelbach, Pfalz, along with his wife Catharina Hartmann Jung (1768-1822), made this journey to Crvenka in 1785. The motto of these pioneers was: *Better times will come with the help of the Lord.*

And so it was. In time, Crvenka thrived. They built the Frankenkanal (1792) that connected the rivers Danube and Theiss, which was extremely important to transport the agricultural products, which these people depended upon. The majority of this group of Germans was Protestant or Lutheran. They built a neo-baroque church, which was dedicated on October 11, 1812.

They came to be known as the Donauschwaben (Danube + Swabia, a state in Germany). Culturally they never broke their ties with their mother country, Germany. Politically this area belonged to the Austrian-Hungarian Empire until World War I, when it became Yugoslavia.

Farming was the major source of income, but several factories also played a major role in the modern economy. In 1944 the population rose to 10,000 inhabitants.

The majority of the people lived in peace. They were a small nation, who lived within another country. They would probably have identified themselves as "Crvenkaer"- neither Yugoslavian nor Reichsdeutsche.

It was a good place to call home. I was an only child, born to loving, caring parents. I had wonderful grandparents and many relatives. Besides being affectionate and devoted, my father taught me early in life the value of an education, morality and honesty.

My mother was a very outgoing person. She demanded order and discipline. She always made our home feel very special with her creativity. I feel great devotion to both of my parents.

My maternal grandparents, the Stefans, lived only a few houses away from us. In the same house lived my uncle and aunt, my mother's only sister. Their children, Willi and Elis, were like my siblings. We were one big family. I recall fun-filled summer days and cozy winter evenings. I attended Kindergarten at the age of three, along with my cousins and friends.

The Stefans, my mother's family, had always been in farming, dating back to the founding of Crvenka. Grandfather Stefan took great pride in his family. Since he lost his mother in early childhood, his grandparents raised him. Until they died, they provided for him a few extra years of education. Mathematics was his favorite subject. He was always a willing teacher to his grandchildren whenever we needed extra help with our assignments.

Oma Stefan was always patient and kind. Her energy seemed to endure forever. Many holidays she either bought or knitted identical dresses for Elis and me. In the evenings she indulged us in telling fairy tales, only twice, which was her limit. Then we had to close our eyes and go to sleep.

In the summertime we accompanied her to the vineyard and the fruit orchard. There she showed us how a big rhubarb leaf could be a great umbrella and how two cherries attached to each other made a splendid earring. She baked the best bread and on wednesdays, when we all went to the open- air market, Elis and I were allowed to pick out one piece of toy pottery, which we carefully took home and placed next to the rest of our collection. She was a great lady.

My father's family, the Jungs, also traced their ancestry back to the early settlement when Michael Johann Jung made the long journey from Frankelbach, Germany to Crvenka. They too had always been in farming.

My Grandfather Jung died in World War I. He was a platoon leader in the Austrian-Hungarian Army. Consequently, I never knew him, but my father had wonderful memories of him. He spoke of the sadness and loss he felt when his father died.

My grandmother Jung had an undying spirit to persevere. She not only lost her husband in World War I, but also her oldest son, who was killed in the same war at the age of 18. Earlier in her life, she also lost several babies in infancy.

Grandmother Jung remarried after her three remaining children were grown and became grandmother Goetz. After the death of her second husband, she sold their home and his furniture business. In 1942 my parents built a new house and she moved in with us. Together she and I shared a bedroom. Her faith, family and friends were her priorities in life. She was always on the go and I usually accompanied her.

She was always full of surprises. They came in various forms. In the late summer afternoons we often shared a pretzel or some pastry at a coffee shop, or she would buy new lace for a doll bed, or she often took me to the Kristkindlmarkt to admire all the new Christmas displays. I loved her dearly.

On May 6, 1941 German troops marched into Yugoslavia and thus we were all thrown into the winds of World War II. Our daily lives were not affected much in the beginning. Men were drafted and the traffic became greater with more and more German soldiers in town.

The Communists began guerilla warfare. I thought our town was safe. Mother later told me how one night our town was surrounded by guerilla soldiers. They planned to burn the town and kill us all. Fortunately the plot was discovered in time and we were all safe.

The changes in our town mirrored the changes I was going

through when I moved from Kindergarten to first grade.

Kindergarten was songs, stories and laughter. Our teachers were

young, pretty and fun to be with. They were nurturing and helpful,

especially when you were the only one without a chair in games

like musical chairs.

Our elementary school was huge, dark and cold. The wooden

floors were always polished and squeaked when stepped upon.

Once our teacher stepped into the classroom a frightening silence

hung over the room. He was old, stern and ready to swing the

whip - not only when a pupil misbehaved, but also when he or she

gave the wrong answer. I always breathed a sigh of relief when

either the school bell ended the day or the blaring siren announced

an air raid. Either way we ran like bandits to the safety of our

homes.

As the war continued, the bombing in the big cities intensified

significantly. At the sounds of the sirens all public buildings,

including our first grade, closed and the public took refuge. My mother and I took cover under the fruit trees in our orchard. It was

a frightening feeling, looking at a warm summer sky, loaded with

roaring humming bombers heading for the big cities. The noonday

sun shining on those planes made the entire sky appear like a huge

gray metal sheet, that could drop on us any moment. I had just

begun first grade in 1944 and I clung tightly to my mother's hand

in fright.

As the summer of 1944 was coming to an end, so changed our

daily lives. All males up to age 55 were drafted. Of course, the

younger ones were already in the service or dead. Refusal was not

an option. Those who refused to enlist had a number of problems

to deal with. Their windows were broken, graffiti was written on

their homes, and their children were expelled from school. At first

my uncle objected to joining the army, but after enduring all the

above mentioned indignities, he was ultimately arrested, marched

to the courthouse, and with a gun held to his back, became a

drafted soldier of the Third Reich. Shortly after this, my father also

had to take his place in the ranks of the army. He understood the gravity of the situation at that point and didn't risk refusing. All summer he and some of the men from the neighborhood listened to various forbidden stations on the radio and thus had a better understanding of what was really happening.

It was a sad day when my father, along with a train load of new recruits, stood on the steps of the train as it pulled out waving good-bye with tears in his eyes. He did not know that this would be his final farewell to his home.

The new recruits were shipped from one town to the next for basic training. Families were permitted to visit their men on sundays. Every weekend I went with my mother and her friend, whose husband was also a soldier in this unit, to visit my father. The soldiers wore uniforms made out of rough, cheap fabrics. Only one weapons was issued to several soldiers. It was so good to see him, even if he hugged me in this scratchy uniform. I always looked forward to the next weekend.

Common sense must have told the citizens that the situation in the area was deteriorating, but they also knew that public discussions were not permitted. On one of our visits, my father told my mother, privately of course, that the situation with us was grim. If we were ordered to evacuate we should not hesitate to follow orders, in the hope that when sanity returned to this insane world, we would be reunited some day, some place.

The summer of 1944 brought the constant movement of German troops as well as a stream of refugees from Banat and Romania. They came by the hundreds with horses and covered wagons, leaving their homes to save their lives from the Russians. We gave refuge to many. Listening to their tales of horror was a warning of what was to come for us. The only crime these people had committed was the fact that they were of German descent.

Chapter II

The evacuation

*A*nd so it happened. In the dark of the early morning hours, on the night of October 8, loud knocks on our window awoke us from our sleep. It was an unusually frightening sound and I could hear men's voices coming from the usually quiet, empty street. They sounded authoritative and serious. Mother opened the windows and spoke to two soldiers, who told us to evacuate our town by noon.

All the lights came on everywhere. We dressed quickly and ran a few houses down the street to my grandparents' house. Since my dad was drafted, Grandfather was now the final authority. Their house was also lit and Grandfather had already made the decision that we would all pack and leave as ordered. He had been a Russian prisoner of World War I and was afraid of them. We children did not know who those fearsome Russian soldiers were, but I remember hurrying back home and helping my mother pack.

Every drawer and closet door was unlocked and opened. Mother was in a state of disbelief. She rushed from one place to the next, not really packing, but running to the window and talking to the passers-by, asking what their thoughts were on this whole situation. In the end, my mother and grandmother packed clothes for all of us, including some for my father and a few necessities, like eating utensils and some food. Apparently she took some money when she sold some of the fall harvest. She also packed my small plate, which I had ever since I can remember. It was blue with bold flowers of blue and red painted in the middle. She also packed linens from her dowry which were used later to barter for food. Since the landowners had wagons and horses, they were asked to limit the packages and take as many people as possible. Grandfather filled the bottom of our wagon with suitcases, bundles and trunks and we sat on top of them.

I packed a small leather bag with my beloved teddy bear and a few books. The bear was medium size, dark brown, soft and cuddly. He was my favorite friend, especially for a tea party and quiet play.

Utter chaos ruled. No one doubted this event would happen, but we didn't want to believe it. The town square was the real source of news and from there it was announced that the public should leave, for safety reasons, to flee from the Russians and the Tito Partisans. We were told to go a few miles toward Hungary and wait there. Germany would deliver new weapons in a few weeks and would be victorious. They promised our safety and that our homes would be returned to us.

Not knowing what to believe, the townspeople sought advice from each other. The square was crowded with weeping, shouting, and confused people. The German soldiers were also leaving. Some people were already lined up in their horse-drawn wagons, packed with people and a few belongings, ready to depart. Others were still in disbelief. After all, this land had belonged to the German Donauschwaben for over 150 years. They had earned it with their sweat and their sacrifices. This was the only home they had ever known for generations and generations. The fields, orchards, and vineyards had blessed them with rich harvests. This was not their war. Where would they go? What would become of them?

A few years earlier they had celebrated the 150th anniversary of the town's founding. October 8th, the day of the evacuation, was also the anniversary of the dedication of our Lutheran Church. It was always a special holiday. The town square was turned into a big fairground, with all kinds of rides, music and best of all lots of candy, but not on this day.

My grandfather, who had escaped Russia as prisoner of war in World War I, did not hesitate to leave. He knew life under Russian rule would not be worth living. He was a proud man and loved his home. It hurt him deeply to have to make this drastic decision. He carried his house key, the large vineyard keys and a picture in his pocket until the day he died.

Ironically, most people took great care in leaving their homes scrubbed clean and orderly, like one would be going on a long journey. The animals were fed, the brickyards were swept and the front doors were locked.

October 8, 1944
On Sunday, Oct. 8, at 12 o'clock we left our
beautiful homeland.

Grandpa hitched two horses to his wagon. We gathered a few

belongings and drove to the town square to take our place behind a

long row of wagons ready to move out. The occupants in our

wagon were: my maternal grandparents Stefan, my Aunt Lisi, very

pregnant with her third child, her two children Willi and Elis, my

fraternal grandmother Goetz, and a friend, Tante Juli, my

mother and I. The space was snug, but my cousins and I were

filled with excitement, because we were embarking on an

adventure, so we thought.

At 12 o' clock on that Sunday morning we left our town.

Headed by German officers and soldiers, our wagon train headed

toward Germany. Our pet Dachshund followed for a few days, but

we couldn't take animals with us and he disappeared. That was

devastating for me.

After a few days, everyone who desired to leave had the opportunity to do so. Some, clinging to a few earthly belongings and holding their children in their arms, lined up on the main roads, begging for a generous soul to offer them a ride. Others had a chance to flee by train or boats. Thanks to the help of our Lutheran minister, two ships came to our canal and rescued hundreds of people by taking them to safety up the Danube River to Vienna, Austria. Still others preferred to stay in their homes than to face an uncertain future on the road. Unfortunately, most of them died agonizing deaths.

Chapter III

Our journey through Hungary and Austria

ur long column of wagons was rolling through Hungary and Austria. In the evenings we stopped and slept in public buildings such as schools, theaters, and sometimes inns if they were available. If this was not possible, our rest stops at the end of the day were ditches along the side of the roads. It was now early fall. The cold dew covered our faces and our blankets. The roads were dusty and dirty and smelled of decay and death. We saw dead bodies, dead animals and broken down wagons.

What a contrast to my warm and cozy home! I couldn't help longing to be back in my old room. In the fall and winter, when the clock on the wall announced bedtime, the whole room was wrapped in the warmth of the glowing fire in the Kachelofen, a type of fireplace. I remember this peaceful feeling of falling asleep while watching the shadows of the last red flames dancing on the white ceiling.

On one particular occasion we woke up in a ditch next to dead bodies. Since lights were forbidden in the evenings because of air attacks, when our wagons stopped for the night, we didn't know that a group of people had been shot there and left in the ditches. All of them were men. Someone said they were Jews. It was a horrible, frightening experience. Everyone was in shock wondering, "Are we to have the same fate?"

At times it was truly a test of survival. The very old and the very young were affected the most. Food was scarce. Sometimes we only had one meal a day. Many towns showed unfavorable hospitality toward the endless rows of wagon trains coming through day after day. It seemed that we sat forever on these wagons crowded with tired, hungry people. To stop alone and rest was out of the question because no one wanted to lose his spot in the long column of wagons. We were truly on the run for our lives. The fact that there were so many of us gave us a feeling of security.

In the midst of this turmoil of masses of people and the constant movement from one town to the next, my greatest fear was getting separated from my mother and my family on that wagon. Cold and hunger was one thing, but being all alone on the side of a crowded highway without a family member to care for me or love me would have been totally unbearable. Also as a child I always knew that I could find my home if someone would help me, but now my home no longer existed. That was a cold feeling.

On one particular day, we were so hungry that all three of us children were crying, for we had no food. Grandma Stefan took off her dirty stockings at one of our stops, went to a house and traded them for a loaf of bread. Afterwards, she cried saying, "A short time ago we had so much. Now we don't even have a single loaf of bread to feed our children!"

October 9
From Sombor to Beston I met my husband Heinrich at the edge of the woods. He stayed with us until Beston. Then he had to leave us and we went to Dunafoldvár. There we arrived in the evening at 9 o'clock.

Military personnel and civilians traveled the roads day and night. My father's battalion was passing us in an army truck. I still remember seeing him standing at the end of the truck, holding onto the back end. Mother shouted and he was allowed to stay with us for a short time. It was so good to be with him.

October 13 (Friday)
We crossed the Danube. Then we traveled to Devescer, then Kolentar.

October 18
In the evening at 7 o'clock we arrived here (Kolentar) and we have to stay here to wait out things.

Mother must have still had a small spark of hope to return to her home. Even though everything looked so hopeless, she still held on to her dream. Perhaps that short meeting with my father gave her courage.

October 21

We bought a cow. Later we bought a second one with 380 Pönge (6 Pönge per Kilo). From a forester we bought wood for 500 Pönge.

Flour—80kg. 1 Pönge 80 (per pound)

Sugar—16 deca for one month.

I believe this amount of food was for many families.

October 27

We received 10 kg flour, dried onions and coffee. In Veszprem we received black coffee, marmalade, and lard.

November 1

I received 10 Pönge for Anni and me.

(I assume some of these gifts were rations the German government gave to all the refugees).

November 5

Margarete Diener was born in the hospital in Devescer. After an eight-day stay at the hospital, my sister and her baby came back to us in Kolentar. There a widow named Josephine Holzer accommodated us. When the baby was ten days old, we had to continue our journey.

My Aunt Lisi, my mother's only sister gave birth to a sweet little baby girl. She was called Gretl, which is short for Margarete. We all shared in the joy of having her!

November 10
We butchered a second cow, which was bought for 420 Pönge (5 Pönge per kg). Each person received half a kg of meat.

November 14
We left Kolentar and went to Sopron.

From October 18-November 14 we had a warm place to stay and normal food to eat, as mentioned above in the diary. Grandma Goetz and I slept in the laundry and we were grateful for such luxury. For a short time life was almost normal, at least for us children. We had food to eat and a warm bed to sleep in at night.

November 15

We traveled through rain and snow. It was very cold. We stayed overnight on the open road and we were freezing cold. In the morning we continued our travel. The horses were shaking from the cold. My sister Lisi, after giving birth ten days earlier, was sitting in the back of the wagon. We received 3 kg coffee, marmalade, and some sugar. We were all frozen. It was very cold, but the sun was shining.

November 17

It was a cold and cloudy day. At 8 o'clock in the evening we crossed the border to Austria, to a sugar factory. We almost had an accident. (Grandfather almost lost control of the wagon, when the lights and the noise of a group of trucks scared the tired animals.) *We continued seven km farther until 10 o'clock. We slept at Brüdersdorf.*

November 18
We continued to travel. There was a big air attack at noon. Then we stood four hours in the freezing cold. That evening we had a warm room at an inn.

The air attacks were quite frequent. The planes went mostly to the big cities, but later they targeted the civilian wagon columns also. Since we were on the open road and had no shelter to take refuge from these bombers, we usually took cover in cornfields. I remember lying face down in those rain-soaked fields, heavy with the smell of autumn's decay. I was listening to the deadly roaring of the enemy planes, closing my eyes and waiting for them to disappear. Mother was always next to me and I felt a beacon of security and hope.

November 19
We received four buckets of oats for the horses, one kg butter, three loaves of bread, and one and a half kg lard.

November 20
There was a big air attack again. In the evening we slept at a "Busta" (farm).

November 21
We received one loaf of bread and half a sausage. The next evening we stayed at a Heim (German cultural center). *We received sausage, bread, and warm tea. We left in the morning.*

November 22
We arrived in St. Pölten; stayed overnight in a coffee house.

November 23
At noon we gave our horses to the Wehrmacht (Wehr=defense and Macht=power). Mother wept. The horses were her last bond to her home and land.

Our goal was to be safe from the Russian troops and Tito's Communists. It was now late in the fall and the weather continued to create problems. Food, once again, was rationed for both humans and animals. The horses became exhausted from lack of food and the cold. Some nights we slept under the open sky on fairgrounds. It was freezing cold. We took refuge under the wagons from the freezing rain and wind.

Necessity is the mother of all inventions. During these times of trial, the men helped each other to construct covers for their wagons - just like the American pioneers had traveling West. Only our journey came to an end late in November. As mentioned before, we gave our horses and wagons to the German army, a branch of the German military forces (Wehrmacht), in exchange for a train ride to Germany – destination unknown.

Chapter IV

Our flight to Germany

November 24-25

We stayed overnight in a gymnasium at a school.

November 25

Our luggage was transported by truck to a freight train at noon. (We still had about one large suitcase for each person)

November 27

In the morning at 7 we were settled into the train and left at 12 o'clock noon. We left for Glatz.

November 28- 29

We traveled by day and night in a freight car. The weather was extremely cold.

November 29

We stayed overnight at an inn in Bolgenheim.

November 30

Continued our journey to Kunzendorf. At 12 o'clock at night we stayed at an inn. There we stayed until December 5. Then we were taken to private homes. We stayed with a lady whose name was Martha Schmidt, but we were eating at the inn. There are 68 people from Crvenka here at the inn.

December 24

We were distributed to more private homes. Anni, Mother Goetz, and I received a small warm room with a family by the name of Engel.

December 27

We received our food rationing cards. Some left. Still with us are:

Paul Stefan and wife (my parents)

Franz Klees with wife, daughter-in-law

Juli Diener with daughter and children

Juli Welsch (our neighbor, who left home with us)

Phillip Braun

Anna Judt with children

Käthe Jung and child (my mother and I)

Katarina Goetz (my fraternal grandmother)

Lisi Diener with children (my aunt and cousins, Willi, Elis and Baby Gretl)

Juli Weiss and daughter

Dinga Becker and son

Wilmos Jung, wife, daughter, her mother and 4 children

Schäfer seven persons

Rosalia Meyer

Jakob Siegel

Adam Wagner and wife

Magdalena Will

Georg Scheidt and wife

Today was the first time we bought our food with the rationing cards.

January 8, 1945

I received rationing stamps for shoes and stockings. I bought shoes for Anni for 15 Mark and one pair of shoes for 12 Mark for me.

January 13

In Bolgenheim I bought:

A bucket

One spoon

One pot- 2 Mark

One glass bowl

One pair of stockings

One suitcase — 7 Mark

After giving up our horses, we continued our travel to eastern Germany. It was now winter. Cold and misery followed us.

We had a small pot-bellied stove in the center of our freight car in the train. Whenever the train stopped for a moment, Grandpa and other adults searched for scraps of wood along the train stations. In this manner we kept from freezing. My mother gave us a cold sandwich occasionally. That was our food.

We slept on top of the luggage, which was piled up high, next to a small opening, near the ceiling. As our train roared through cities and small towns at dusk, loaded with hundreds of refugees, we could see lamps glowing in windows. I always tried to imagine how these families were so blessed to live in a warm home with hot food to eat and a cozy bed to sleep in.

Finally my wish was granted. We landed in Kunzendorf, in the county of Glatz in lower Silesia in the eastern section of Germany. It was Christmas time. The village was nestled in the beautiful snow covered mountains of the Riesengebirge. It truly looked like a Christmas scene. The sights and the sounds of the war were almost forgotten. The familiar old Christmas carols filled the air at the inn. I remember big baskets full of red apples were our presents and the taste of those apples could not have compared to the finest chocolates in the world. The basic goodness of humanity reached out at such a moment and people shared love and kindness. It was indeed a time of brief contentment.

My mother, Grandmother Goetz, my Aunt Käthe and I lived in a small room on a large dairy farm.

My Aunt Käthe was my father's sister, who also left Crvenka with a group of neighbors the same day we left. During the journey she became seriously ill due to a severe fall. Luckily she was able to locate us and reunite with us in Kunzendorf. Again, for a short time, life was almost normal. Even though my Aunt Käthe was very ill she was so kind and patient and spent many afternoons teaching me to read, since we did not have any schools.

The realities of the war quickly swept over us. News of losses and retreats of the German army reached our little village. At nights the horizon appeared as a flaming fire. Our windows and doors rattled from the vibrations of the bombing of the cities, night after night. Later we found out this was the battle of Breslau. Again many refugees came from the East. Some barely escaped with their lives. They came in droves with small children and old people, some barely able to travel. They were scared, hungry and cold. All searched for safety from the horrors of this war. The Russians were steadily advancing and once again, we had to make a decision to run to a safer place.

Grandmother Goetz and my Aunt Käthe stayed behind. At this point my aunt was too weak to travel. They were transported by a hospital train to Zittau, where my aunt died. However, they escaped the approaching Russians. From then on we remained separated from my grandmother.

Chapter V

The end of World War II

February 13, 1945
We left Kunzendorf in the evening and went to Märzendorf. We slept at the train station over night.

February 14
At 9 o'clock in the morning we went to Landshut. There we left at noon and traveled until 5 in the evening to Freudenau. We slept in a movie theater.

February 15
We left Freudenau.

February 16
We received food in the morning. Then at 9 o'clock we were in Prague.

February 17
At midnight we arrived at Bendorf and traveled another 3 kilometers to Frauenreuth (Sudetenland, later part of Czechoslovakia). At an inn we received warm soup and boiled potatoes

with salt. We stayed at a school over night. In the morning we received bread and coffee. Then we were distributed into private homes. We lived in the house of a seamstress whose name was Gretel Haselbauer. We shared two rooms with 13 people.

February 18
We picked up our luggage at a train station 5 kilometers away from here. My father fell out of the train while unloading a sack of flour. He broke his arm.

It took Grandpa Stefan's arm a long time to heal, since it was difficult to find medical help in this small town.

February 19
We have a warm room and we are all cooking together.

March 1

I received 40. Mark for Unterhaltsvorschuß (living expenses).

Again we traveled by train along with hundreds of other refugees from all over. We slept in various places as mentioned above, and ate whatever was available. Finally we found a safe haven in Frauenreuth, north of Eger in the Sudetenland (Czech Republic).

We were fortunate not to have lived in a big city. Out in the country we had plenty of potatoes. Thanks to the skill of the cooks in our small group, we never went to bed hungry. It was spring again. The meadows were green and the fruit trees in the orchards were covered with blossoms. We even had a school again for the first time since we left Crvenka, but only for a short time.

During the winter and early spring of 1945, the bombings were unending. The shattering of the windows and the flashings of lights came nightly. It was like a huge thunderstorm that hovered over us as if to swallow up the entire world.

The wounded German soldiers, often in very small groups, passed through this town daily. They were mostly very young boys retreating from the advancing American forces.

May 6, 1945

In the evening at 8 o'clock we were captured by the Americans in Frauenreuth. We were 32 persons together in the basement. The soldiers were two men. They were very friendly. We continued to receive groceries through our rationing cards.

All during that day of May 6, the fighting became intense. Everyone was ordered to take cover in the basements. My mother, distrustful of the safety of the structure of this old house, had us take refuge in the orchard and lie face down to escape the flying bullets. Grandfather came with us and finally, when the fighting intensified, we joined the rest in the basement.

In the evening of that day the American tanks rolled into the village. Earlier during the day, pamphlets were distributed through the village instructing the public that every house must hang a white sheet on the front of the house, as a sign of surrender. It also warned us that in the event that any weapons or ammunitions were found in any house, all occupants would be shot on the spot. We were frightened, but at the same time, we were grateful that the Americans, instead of the Russians, were coming.

Two American soldiers came to our basement door with loaded weapons and ordered us to line up in front of the house, with our arms up in the air. We were mostly children, women and a few old people like my grandparents. This non-threatening sight moved one of the soldiers with compassion. He sat down on the basement step, took off his helmet, wiped the sweat off his brow and inquired, in perfect German, if we were hungry and in need of food. This was unbelievable! Only moments ago, we feared for our lives, and the two soldiers, who were our enemy only a few hours before, were not only kind, but also concerned about our well-being. Needless to say everyone was grateful and amazed.

The streets were covered with American soldiers in tanks and trucks. Some of the vehicles were decorated with fresh green tree branches and flowers. Some of the local girls joined the soldiers and sat on top of the tanks.

Grandfather was complaining about these girls who, only one day ago, accompanied the retreating German soldiers to the edge of the town. Now they were welcoming the Americans. He could not understand how proper girls could behave in such a manner.

May 10, 1945
The war is over.

Since the war was now over, at least for us, the people emerged from their shattered lives and tried to piece their world back together. We, of course, wanted to go back home to Yugoslavia. Home was Crvenka, the place where we left our houses, fields and belongings. That was the place where our ancestors were born and where we cultivated the land for generations.

We did not know where my father or uncle were, or if they were still alive, but we were hopeful. Hope burns like a lone candle in the darkness of night and promises the sunrise to come.

And so with great hope and enthusiasm we inquired about a
homeward journey.

Chapter VI

Our homeward journey to Crvenka, Yugoslavia

May 23

We received permission to begin our homeward journey.

June 14

We received our permit in Falgenau in Sudetenland (Czechoslovakia).

June 17

At 6 o'clock in the morning we left Frauenreuth with a wagon and went to Kalsbad. At 3 o'clock in the afternoon, we were placed into a transport train and left at 7 in the evening and rode to Pilsen.

June 19

We arrived at a Pilsener suburb at 4 o'clock in the afternoon. Then we went to the Yugoslavian council and asked for permission to begin our homeward journey.

June 20

At 7 o'clock in the evening we left Pilsen with a Yugoslavian permit.

June 22

We crossed the Czech border at 4 o'clock in the morning.

June 23

We arrived at 4 in the morning in Vienna. We stayed in Strashof in the train for three days.

June 26

At 2 o'clock in the morning we continued our journey for half an hour, then we stopped between stations. This is the way it went every day. Then we stopped at Horgos. The Yugoslavian Partisans came and inspected our train, which was loaded with Donauschwaben. Then they sent us back to Melykút (Hungary). We stayed there in the *train for ten days. Then we were sent back to Baja across the Danube to Wiener Neustadt* (Austria).

Many of our people thought naively, that we should be allowed to return to our homeland. They did not know that Tito's Communists, called Partisans, were now in control of Yugoslavia and they had already decided as far back as 1943, to eliminate all Donauschwaben, ethnic Germans.

Our train eventually reached its destination within a few miles of Crvenka, our hometown. The Partisans, as stated in my mother's diary, refused to let us come back and they sent us back to Hungary.

From June 17 to August 2 a railroad box car was our home. Several families were packed into a single car. We again slept on top of our luggage. Whatever we could barter, beg, or steal was our source of food. Money was worthless. A pot placed over two bricks on an open fire was our kitchen.

My mother, dressed in a dark summer dress, barefooted and with her thick dark hair pinned to the back of her head into a bun, was our chief provider. She left the train station early every morning and usually returned with some sort of food.

Occasionally when a stranger asked her what nationality she was, because of her appearance and her dark tanned skin, she would say without hesitation, "Gypsy!" In her mind, she could, no doubt, relate to Gypsies. She was homeless and had to fight daily for herself and her family for the basic human needs of existence.

Often Grandfather would go with Mother to find food, but because of a severe hernia, he could not carry much. Also it was customary for the train to move a few miles up or down the track without notice. Mother could run faster than Grandfather. There was always the fear of becoming separated

Grandmother and my Aunt Lisi took care of the rest of us children. My aunt's baby was sick most of the time. There was neither medical help nor medicine for the refugees. Many days we didn't think the baby would live. The heat in the railroad cars was terrible and the nourishment for babies was hard to find.

Occasionally the Russian soldiers came with burlap sacks filled with dried pieces of old leftover bread. Even though it was hard as a rock and usually had teeth marks showing, we ate it gratefully. Nothing was ever wasted, because after we had eaten, the soldiers came and collected the leftovers for the nourishment of the next group of starving refugees.

The Russians occupied Hungary. Along the railroads and at different stations was a great confusion with masses of people. There were long trains of Russian soldiers including many female soldiers, refugees and German prisoners of war. The German prisoners were cramped into these trains and locked in tightly.

The sun shone unmercifully onto these masses of humanity. The odor of sweat, urine, and death was terrifying. At night the dead bodies were removed before the trains continued their journey to Russia and forced labor camps.

Some of the prisoners dropped slips of paper through the cracks of the carts, stating their names, hometowns, and vital statistics, and asking the finders of these papers to pass this information on to their families. We helped Grandfather, along with some other men, to collect the papers and place them into his coat pockets for future reference. My uncle or father could very well have been in any one of these trains. We did not know if they were dead or alive.

Meanwhile the Russian soldiers partied heartily and their shouting and singing could be heard until dawn. The refugees were at their mercy. Jewelry was among the most sought-after items. Women hid their wedding rings, earrings and watches. My mother placed her jewelry into a small sack and pinned it inside her underwear for safekeeping.

Many other stories of injustice circulated and it was just common sense that at night women sought safety by hiding to avoid being raped. Jewelry was never worn. There simply wasn't any law to protect us.

Chapter VII

Kaisersteinbruck– a barbed wire refugee camp in Austria

The denial to go back home was painful to our people, but at that moment we did not realize that it was a blessing in disguise. Some refugees were permitted to enter Yugoslavia, but were placed into concentration camps, where many died.

We lived in a train in Hungary all summer and when fall came the Russians placed us into a Russian concentration camp in Austria.

August 2
A refugee camp in Kaisersteinbruck.
We are living in a small room with the Jakob Stefan Family. (There were about 20 people in this room.)

Originally the camp was a training center for the soldiers of the Kaisers. The camp consisted of many barracks, with a main street leading to the officer's building of the Red Army. It stood on a hill and was crowned with a big red neon light of the hammer and sickle that lit the camp day and night. Behind the building was a hospital for the Russian soldiers and for us civilians. Armed guards and a barbed wire fence surrounded the entire camp.

The ultimate goal was to eliminate as many people as possible. In the beginning we lived in a big room of about thirty to forty persons. Later, as mentioned in the diary, we lived in a small room with about twenty people. TB and malnutrition were the main causes of death. Again the very young and the very old were the largest casualties.

Once a day we had to line up in front of a mess hall and everyone received a cup of soup, which was mostly some sort of liquid with little pieces of vegetables floating on top. The small children and babies had a separate line and they received a cup of porridge. My cousins and I were nine and seven by now and did not qualify for the "Porridge Line." Every day when my baby cousin finished eating her porridge, one of us took turns in licking out her cup. We were so hungry.

Several times we were woken during the night by the guards and marched to the barracks where the showers were located. Inside, the doors were locked and after waiting for water and soap, which never came, we were told to march back to our rooms.

In hindsight, it must have been a scare tactic similar to what the Nazis did to the Jewish people. In any case, we obviously were never executed nor did we have water and soap for a bath.

Meanwhile our clothes were randomly thrown into big containers, which in turn were placed into a huge oven in order to disinfect our clothes from lice and bed bugs. Unfortunately, the oven was not hot enough to destroy the pests, and bugs were crawling over all the clothes when we got them back. In the end, those of us who did not have any bugs became infested with them.

Every morning medical personnel walked through each room looking for sick people. Any person who was unable to get out of bed was ordered to go to the hospital, from which no one ever returned. My mother had an uncle, who died under these circumstances.

August 25
Uncle Christian Diener died at 10 o'clock this morning.

August 26

The funeral was this evening. Relatives who were there were:

Paul Stefan (my grandfather and brother-in –law of the deceased)

Kathe Jung (my mother)

Heinrich Diener

Christian Diener

Jakob Stefan

Lenka Stolz

And several other Crvenkaer. The minister was a Lutheran minister from Torschau (a neighboring town from Crvenka).

Several people from Crvenka sang a few songs.

September 4

Japan capitulated to Russia.

Many people died. The rules in the camp became somewhat lax. In spite of the barbed wired fences, the starving people found ways to get food. We found wild onions in the woods in the back of the barracks. During the nights, when the guards were not looking, a few people at a time crawled through holes at specific spots. Once outside they found some food, if nothing but potatoes left from the harvest.

On one of those escapes we went to a farmhouse where some relatives who were also refugees lived. They had food and gave me an entire small loaf of bread to eat all by myself! Never was a gift more generous or precious!

We always had to return to our camp because every person was required to have a card of identification listing where he lived. Without a card, the Russians would have arrested us and sent us to another refugee camp.

October 15
We left the camp at 12 o'clock heading toward Vienna. We stayed overnight at a Busta (farm) with a relative Adam Dautermann. On the next day we went to a different place. There we waited all night in a ditch.

October 16

We went to a house and spent the night with a lady. In the morning we left and had to go back to the camp. Before we left we received food and while we were out of the camp, we had three meals that day.

Apparently that was one of the escapes from the camp in order to find some food.

It seemed as if we lived in this camp for an eternity, at least in the eyes of a child, but according to the diary we lived there only three and a half months. Once again, like left over goods, the Russians didn't know what to do with us. This time they sent us to the Soviet Zone of Germany.

Chapter VIII

The Soviet Zone of Germany

November 15

At 11 o'clock in the morning we left the camp of Kaisersteinbruck and went to Wilhelmsdorf. There at 12 o'clock at night, we were placed into cargo wagons at the train station.

November 16

We left at 10 o'clock for Vienna. Then Prague, Dresden, Schwerin, and Schwaan. We arrived on November 23. We found refuge in a fish factory, where the Germans there gave us food and shelter.

Several families were squeezed into a dirty, cold box car on a train along with many hundreds of other refugees. We had no heat and very little food. After a week, we arrived in Mecklenburg, East Germany.

November 27

At noon we left Schwaan and went to Vorbeck. There we found room at an inn. Three times a day we received food from different farm families, who took turns feeding us in this camp.

December 14

We were distributed to different private farmhouses. I went with my parents, Anni, my sister Lisi with her three children and Fritz Pfister and family went to a farm belonging to the family of Otto Maier. We received food rationing cards, but one can buy bread only once a week; 1 kg for me and ½ kg for Anni.

We shared a small room, a former servant's quarters, with the people mentioned above. We slept on straw covered with blankets. In the morning the straw was swept aside, so that the room was big enough to hold so many people.

Besides the bread, which we received through rations, our main diet consisted of potatoes and red salt, animal salt in the shape of big blocks. Occasionally we had milk, but days passed before we even tasted meat, which was usually found in soups.

The situation in the Soviet Zone of Germany was quite hopeless. The farmers had only a minimum of livestock and only the necessary grain to sustain their existence. They buried most of their valuable possessions and even hid some of their smaller animals in the woods. The farmers dug holes in the middle of the woods, and placed animals like pigs or sheep in the dugout. Thus covered with tree branches, the animals were safe. The Russians never bothered to venture into the woods. Sometimes at night the Russian soldiers came with large trucks and took whatever they needed.

The stores in the towns were boarded up. If the stores still had windows, they displayed some things that were available for barter.

We simply existed from day to day. There were other refugees from all over and we were all stuck in this area, not knowing were my father, my uncle or the rest of our relatives were.

January 25, 1946
Annchen (Anni) had an operation on her arm.
The doctor had to use anesthetics. It was five
kilometers to the doctor in town.

I was malnourished and became very ill. My entire body was covered with sores and a serious infection localized on the outside of the elbow of my upper arm. Grandmother Stefan and my mother pulled me in a little hand wagon through the woods on a 5-kilometer journey to a doctor, who opened up the skin to release the infection. Since not much medicine was available, the doctor instructed my mother to bring a few tablespoons of lard into which the nurse mixed some powder to create a healing cream, which brought me back to health.

I remember sleeping a lot. In the middle of the night as the wind was howling and blowing against our little windows, I could hear the barking of a dog here and there in the distance.

March 9

Our mother (Grandmother Goetz) *came to us from Flemendorf. Then I went with her to Vorbeck to pick up her baggage. That was 148 kilometers away.*

Many people became separated, so for my grandmother to find us was a small miracle. It was a great joy for all of us to be reunited once again. My mother went with her to get her baggage. The lady of the house was happy to accompany my mother and grandmother since she wanted to visit relatives in Vorbeck and it was not safe for a woman to travel alone. This entire area was in the Soviet Zone. Along with personal possessions, the safety of the citizens was at great risk from Russian attack. Of course she jumped at the chance to go with them.

As the ladies stepped into the train, which was crowded with Russian soldiers, one of the female soldiers spotted the fox boa Mrs. Maier was wearing. The soldier demanded Mrs. Maier hand it over but she refused. This angered the soldier, and she went into a seizure. At this point they all knew they were in big trouble. In the midst of this confusion, my grandmother wrapped the fur around her waist underneath her coat. They also knew they had to get out of there fast. They pulled scarves around their faces in the hope of concealing their identity and hurried to the first exit to leave the train at the next station. Just as they had feared, the Russian soldier stood at the exit gate, accompanied by two male soldiers searching for the ladies with the fur. Luckily the fur was safe under Grandmother's coat and the soldiers could not spot the ladies.

One day early that spring, my Aunt Lisi received a letter from her husband in Munich, the American Zone in the West, stating that he was alive and looking for his family. Most letters were passed on by person-to-person contact. The Red Cross was also tremendously helpful in reuniting families, but they were totally overburdened with the volume of refugees. So a letter from my uncle was a double joy because not only was he alive, but we also knew where he was!

My uncle's letter was our only passport to freedom - the Western Zone of the American occupation. Without permission from the Russian authorities, no one crossed any of their borders. We were basically stuck in the Soviet Zone. My uncle enclosed a document from the person who was in charge of the refugee camp in Munich, and who also happened to be from our hometown in Crvenka, stating that we had official permission from the Western authorities to come to Munich. This was, of course a fake, but we were able to leave.

Daily, for several weeks, my mother had gone to the local courthouse with the letter and forged document in her pocket, trying to secure permission to cross over to the West. The authorities denied her daily request. Helping a refugee family travel to the other side of war-torn Germany was hardly a priority for the courthouse. Persistence and patience often brought results, however. Finally, after proving that the letter and document were "legitimate", and that she was able to pay for all our train tickets, we were granted a pass to go.

Actually crossing the border from the Russian Zone to the American Zone became another big hurdle. We traveled from Vorbeck, East Germany to Munich, West Germany. The distance between these places is really not far at all, but for a group of civilians to travel, it was a time consuming event. We went from one train to the next, staying in endless refugee camps in between. We were constantly inspected for contagious diseases and lice. Our papers were carefully inspected. The lines of refugees were enormous. It seemed as if everyone was coming and going.

April 6
We were granted departure documents through the police from Vorbeck. And on the seventh in the morning we left Vorbeck in a wagon to Schwaan and then we went to Güstrow.

April 8

In the morning at 7 we left Güstrow, crossed over to Schwerin. In the morning at 9 we arrived in Leipzig. There we stayed overnight at an inn.

April 9

At 7 in the morning we left and arrived later in Erfurt. There we changed trains and arrived that evening at 6 o'clock in Eisenach. There we stayed overnight in a refugee camp.

April 11

We left Eisenach, went to Gotha. We arrived at 8 in the evening. There we stayed in a camp and received food.

April 27

We left Gotha and went by train to Gera, then Eisennach. From Eisenach, leaving at 2 in the afternoon, traveled until 6 in the evening, arrived in Erfurt. There we stayed overnight.

April 28

In the morning at 5:30 we left Erfurt and arrived at 8:30 in the morning at Gera. In the afternoon we went to Weisschlitz, arrived there at 9 in the evening and stayed overnight at the train station.

April 29

At 5 in the evening we left and arrived at 6 in Oelznitz. We stayed in a camp. We were registered and stayed in the camp until May 4.

May 4

We left the camp at 6 o'clock in the morning and were placed into the train at Oelznitz. We were 1500 persons. We went back to Hof. There we were inspected and again deloused and registered once again.

77

May 5

We left Hof in the afternoon and to Regensburg. We arrived there at 9 and stayed overnight in the train station waiting room. We left Regensburg at 6:30 and went to Munich.

Chapter IX

Munich, Germany

May 6

In the evening we went to the Implerlager, a large refugee camp in Munich. I had to pay for food right away. It was 9 Mark and 10 Pfennig per week.

I remember sitting on top of the baggage, which must have been a safe place to set small children down for we were forever sitting on luggage. Perhaps it was also done to keep the luggage safe. We must have looked like a bundle of misery sitting there in the hustle and bustle of that enormous train station on that spring day, May 5, 1946.

My uncle came and took us to the Implerlager, another refugee camp, but this was a good camp. In the camp stood rows of barracks. It seemed that Germany was full of them. Most of the families there were from our hometown, which was in a sense a form of security for most of the people, since they had to face the difficult fact that a return to their home was forever gone. The only spark of hope now was to be reunited with their loved ones, whom they had lost track of during the war.

Several families occupied a single room. The contents of each room consisted of rows of bunk beds, several tables and a few chairs. The trunks and suitcases served as dressers. The walls were bare and were constructed of gray concrete blocks. The wooden floors were scrubbed clean with ashes every week.

The meals were more substantial and for the first time in a long time, we actually had regular medical attention. There were countless lines for x-rays for TB screening, physical exams, and dental check-ups. The three regular meals per day were prepared in huge kettles in the camp kitchen. Everyone was required to pay with money and rationing stamps for these meals.

Every evening each person received an extra slice of bread. My mother, with a big knife and a small scale, was usually the distributor. She carefully cut and weighed each peace of bread, so that everyone received an equal portion.

Potatoes were plentiful. In the center of each room stood a pot-bellied stove with a pot of potatoes simmering on top. Every evening we sat around the table and ate our piece of potato without feeling hunger pains.

Life returned to normal. We had food, shelter and a warm room with clean beds to sleep in. Most of our fathers were still missing. At one point my mother received information from an ex-soldier who said he saw my father fall into a ditch and presumed he was dead since he was in terrible condition. We wept, but still held out hope for his return.

Best of all we had a school and church to go to. By now I was 8 years old and had only a few months here and there of formal first grade education. I finished first grade from May through July. It was very exciting to go to school every day. It was only for a few hours each day since most of the schools had been bombed and the few classrooms remaining had to be shared with so many students. The teachers were kind and encouraging. I loved school and we learned so much in such a short time.

May 16
I began to work at the Red Cross in the
Blutburgerstraße.

Every able-bodied person was required to work. The jobs were
unending. Many people from our camp also worked for the
American GIs. Later my mother also worked there in their food
supply storage.

July 6
My brother-in-law Jakob came back to Munich
from a prison camp.

August 30
I stopped working for the Americans. I received
58 Mark every two weeks.

September 3
I began to work in a shoe factory. I worked from 7
in the morning to 5 in the evening. I received 57
Pfennige per hour. I ate my lunch at noon in the

cafeteria. *I bought a pair of leather shoes for Anni for 15 Mark and one pair for me for 8 Mark, for Christmas. I ended work there at Christmas.*

November 29, 1946
Heinrich (my father) came to us at 12:00 at night.

My father was back! He looked very thin, more serious and a lot older.

Many soldiers returned during the summer of 1946. The joy was echoed through the entire camp when suddenly a husband, son, father, or brother would appear unannounced at the front gate of the camp. In this manner my father also appeared one night. We were all so overjoyed, especially since an eyewitness had told us that he was last seen sitting sick and weak at the edge of a road, unable to walk.

He had been taken prisoner by the Russians in the Soviet Zone of Germany. This group of prisoners had to defuse bombs and work in a stone quarry.

Once a day they received a meager soup. Many men died and some of the more able-bodied prisoners were shipped to Russia to work in the coalmines. The prisoners were marched from one town to the next. Being sick and weak, my father, one of the last prisoners of this march, fell into a ditch from exhaustion. Eventually he found his way to a farm and the farm woman nursed him back to health in exchange for helping her with her farm work. He always claimed it was not only the kindness of that woman, it was the fresh country air and the raw eggs, which he consumed while collecting the daily eggs, that gave him back his health.

He had searched for us, not knowing where we were or if we were dead or alive. For the last two years we had had no contact. Mother had kept close contact with relatives and friends in other places. We had even gone to different train stations hoping to find someone who had any knowledge of the where-abouts of my father. Like so many other families, a friend gave my father our address.

My father never talked much about the two years he had been separated from us. I can only imagine what he must have gone through, hearing the stories of many other people and the injustices he suffered.

Basically stripped of their land and all worldly possessions, people were grateful for their lives and those of their family and friends. On Sunday mornings the mess hall became our church. The closest church had been destroyed by the war and not until much later was the chapel rebuilt for worship. Church attendance was great. Hymns had never been sung more sincerely or prayers spoken more gratefully.

This same mess hall served as a dance floor on Saturday nights. It was not difficult to persuade a person with an accordion to play a tune and there was an instant orchestra. The young people sang and danced until the early hours of the morning. It was one of the highlights of the week, when we children could press our noses to the glass of the windows and watch these people dance waltzes and polkas until our parents reminded us that it was bedtime and we had to leave.

Our greatest delight came whenever we spotted a green U.S. Army truck rumbling into our camp. That was like instant Christmas. We ran to greet those nice soldiers and to see what surprises they had for us. The soldiers, amused by our exuberance, distributed sacks of toys, Hershey bars, candy, and always chewing gum. There was always enough to go around from the tiniest to the biggest child. I believe the gift bearers enjoyed this ritual as much as the recipients. They were never in a hurry to leave and we always rewarded them with "danke," big smiles, and waves.

They also brought clothing and food for the adults, but the novelty of the toys and especially the chewing gum, which was a totally foreign thing to us, took top spots. We did not have toys. We either had to leave them behind or they had been lost along the way, like my bag with my teddy bear.

I remember receiving a scrapbook once that pictured aspects of American life. It showed big city streets decorated in Christmas splendor, baseball games and other children's activities. No doubt, some American school children constructed these books to give us a glimpse of America. I tried to imagine what life must be like in a country far away called America.

It was amazing how people, placed into difficult situations, learned quickly to manage so well with so little. Nothing was wasted. Most people became quite creative making something useful from nothing. For example, one of the men collected old tin cans and made them into cookie cutters. In turn he sold them to the housewives.

The white, discarded flour sacks from the American food commissaries were washed, bleached if possible, and ironed. The backside of the sacks became handsome white Sunday shirts for the men. The front side of the sacks, with the big bold letters "Pillsbury's Best," were sewn into underwear. In hindsight, it must have been comical to any English speaking person to see underwear with big black letters on the back fluttering in the wind, hanging on the clothesline.

Some of the most beautiful and even stylish dresses were created from old used fabrics. I especially remember one white summer dress that was sewn for me by my mother's cousin, who was a skilled seamstress. It was created from two old dresses from different fabrics. Next to the collar it had three new shining red buttons. I felt so stylish!

Even new recipes were concocted from the contents of different "care packages." Chocolate chips were a highly treasured item and it was surprising what landed in the dough of a delicious strudel.

Some of us were luckier than others because we also received private packages from relatives in America. I had an Uncle Bill and Aunt Anna, my father's brother and wife who lived in the country in Northern Illinois. They were very generous in supplying us with many of life's necessities, and sometimes with luxuries. One time my aunt sent me a small handball, decorated with the stars and stripes. I was the most popular girl in the camp. That was the only ball in the entire community.

How exciting it was to be notified through the mailman that a U.S. package was waiting for us in another part of the city. It was usually a big square box with a large red stamp on it that said "Gift." Since the word "gift" in German means "poison," needless to say we were a little frightened at first of these "poisoned" packages, but we soon learned what great treasures were hiding inside.

September 5, 1946 – January 20, 1948
Packages from America.

My mother had a detailed list of all the different packages we received. We had special status as refugees coming from borders outside of Germany and were able to receive these packages. They were from government sources, churches, organizations and, of course, from relatives. They were a lifesaver and without them, life would have been a lot more difficult. Commerce was not fully restored and most stores were still boarded up. Therefore, every person was still forced to rely on rationing stamps for his food supply.

In the summer and fall, almost everyone went out into the country on weekends to find fruits and vegetables to round out his meal. The trains were packed with people and the little towns must have shuddered with the massive invasion of these city people.

On one occasion my parents and I took a whole weekend to visit a distant relative, who lived in the country. This family had wealth and status in a big city, but during the war the bombs had damaged their home and the family bakery. This lady now lived on the outskirts of the city in a little garden house. It was a lovely setting of greenery and fragrances from the fruit trees and flowers. It really was much like our home we once had far away

One morning on top of the kitchen table, I saw two striped, ripe, peaches. No one was in sight. And without hesitation I devoured not one but both of these juicy delectable fruits. I was old enough to know better, but to a child, who just faintly remembered what fresh fruit tasted like, the temptation was too great!

I was unaware that these peaches were payment for the hairdresser, who had just finished the lady's hair. I was scolded and reprimanded. Not only had I embarrassed our hostess, but I had also disgraced my parents. Everyone was angry with me, but the hairdresser just laughed. To me the taste of the peaches was worth the humiliation.

The Red Cross and other civic organizations had Christmas parties for the children. We lived in a refugee camp and I believe for that reason, we were treated differently, but it was not bad.

Because of malnutrition and infectious diseases such as TB, we were exposed to what seemed like endless physical exams and chest x-rays. Some of my friends were brought back to health in hospitals. If a child was undernourished, he was sent to a summer day camp. A number of my friends and I usually qualified to the envy of some of our "chubbier" friends. These were fun-filled days with good food, friends and hikes through the woods.

These were happy times, at least to us children. Every fall we marched off to a wonderful school with a book bag, filled with books and school supplies. The routine of daily living replaced all the horrible things we had experienced. The rubble surrounding us was slowly replaced with new buildings and the old historical places were carefully repaired to their former glory.

In 1948 when the Reichsmark was replaced with the Deutsch Mark, a total economic upward movement appeared almost over night. The boarded up stores were reopened with shining glass windows filled with all kinds of merchandise and never-before seen foods. Most were expensive, but at least they were available. No longer did the public need rationing stamps to purchase food or clothing.

Meanwhile we still lived in barracks, only now every family had a separate room to call its own. Our room was our apartment. Everything, with the exception of a bathroom, was in this room. My father, who was a trained carpenter, made white furniture for our room. It was very pretty. Like everyone else, we had a window box with all sorts of beautiful flowers.

Every inch of unused ground in the camp was turned into gardens and flowerbeds. Most people built a small storage shed next to their vegetable garden and planted flowers on the edge. My mother and I picked out flowers and under her guidance I planted my first flower garden. She introduced me to a life-long love for the beauty of flowers.

Everyone searched for a better life. Some left the refugee camp for public housing, which was a slow process since so many native Germans had lost their homes through the bombing and now, with thousands of refugees crowding into West Germany, housing became an acute crisis.

February 5, 1947
Mother (my grandmother Goetz) *left to go to the Funkkaserne.*

May 1, 1947
She left to go to America.

Since my grandmother Goetz had a son, an American citizen living in Illinois, she had priority to immigrate to the USA. The

Funkkaserne was the official military station for the American occupation in our area. It took three months for Grandma to go through political and medical clearance in order to sail to America. All immigrants were required to live in a camp nearby and go through months of medical examinations and political investigations. I was so sad when she left. She was fortunate to embark on the journey to a land of hope and a far better life than what we had, at that time.

Chapter X

Our journey to America

*M*y father began to inquire about immigration possibilities. He had always dreamed of going to America and had lived in Brazil, South America for 11 years prior to his marriage to my mother. He was fearful that sooner or later, if we stayed in Europe, another war could bring us right into a crisis again. He wanted safety and security for his family. Any place but Europe sounded wonderful to him. He was even willing to go back to Brazil. He learned through correspondence with his Lutheran minister in Brazil that the situation there was not favorable either.

After a while he learned that under the Displaced Persons Act our family was eligible to apply to go to the USA. This did not apply to Reichsdeutsche, people born within the borders of Germany, but to people with a foreign pass. With the help of a second cousin who had emigrated just a few years earlier, he found a sponsor for us, the family of Forrest and Naomi Williamson in Haviland County, Ohio. They agreed to provide work for my father. He in turn had to promise to stay with this employer for one year. Our transportation to the United States on an army boat was free, providing we all passed the health and political inquiries.

My father was thrilled and my mother was in tears. In the last seven years she had experienced the loss of her home and property, and all the terrible horrors of war and now, we were finally all alive and safe. Starting all over again, and this time leaving her parents and her sister and family behind, was too much.

At first this American opportunity was planned in secret. I believe my mother thought it probably would not materialize and thus agreed to go. Later my father presented a good case of persuasion to my grandparents and my aunt and uncle and gradually the excitement spread to all.

In the fall of 1951 we left our camp in Munich and moved to a clearing camp provided by the Americans near Dachau. Every morning the GI trucks transported us to the Funkkaserne and we went through our daily rituals of endless lines and many briefings to get political clearance, health exams, shots and vaccinations. In the evenings the same trucks took us back to our sleeping quarters and for evening meals at a mess hall. We even had a crash course in English, of which none of us spoke a word. I recall one especially humorous incident. One of the lesson sheets had the following lines under the title of "Useful Expressions":

"Are you married?"

"Why not?"

I was thirteen at the time and found this very funny. I didn't know how to say, "I am only thirteen and I am sure my parents would frown on a thirteen year old being married!"

By now everyone there was anxious to receive his passport papers, but some were very disappointed when they received their papers of rejection instead. It was sad to see grown people cry. Meanwhile my grandparents Stefan and my Aunt Lisi, Uncle Wilhelm and their three children, my cousins Willi, Elis, and little Gretl, had also applied to go to America.

In the early part of November 1951, we said farewell to everyone and set out on our adventure to America. It was bittersweet to take leave of our relatives and friends and go to an unknown land so far away. Grandmother Stefan cried for days and she knew we would never see each other again. In all my life neither Mother nor I had ever lived farther than a few houses away from my grandparents and my aunt and uncle. My cousins were like the brother and sisters I never had.

On November the 19th we sailed in an American army boat called the Blanchford from the Bremer harbor with a load of about 3000 refugees. The entire process of achieving this moment had taken about two years. My father was deliriously happy. A band on the shore played "Auf Wiedersehen." It was so festive and yet sad at the same time. Some wept and others sang, waving good-bye to Germany, their recent home, and trading this for a life and a land unknown to us.

The voyage was filled with many fall storms. Most of the womens quarters were in the front bow of the ship. Our bedrooms were four floors down and it seemed like we felt every wave of the ocean. Consequently most of us were seasick for the majority of the trip. The waves were enormous. Our little boat was tossed around the Atlantic like a toy in a bathtub.

This ocean crossing experience was definitely military-style. We ate standing up and holding on to large tables. All the men had to help with kitchen duty. Some foods were foreign to us. We always had cold hard-boiled eggs for breakfast. Some time later our daily meals contained a strange substance called "Jell-O" in various colors. Also, we had cards that we could trade for free candy and chocolate bars. Unfortunately, most of us were too sick to eat them.

Finally, after the ten-day trip on the ocean, we arrived late at night in the New York Harbor. Our processing began at five in the morning and by noon we were once again on solid ground, greeted by men and women of the Salvation Army with doughnuts and coffee.

We waited at Grand Central Station in New York and by evening we were placed on a train heading for Ohio. My father had a number of papers hanging on his coat buttons, explaining our destination and the fact that we did not speak English. We were now totally on our own, which was somewhat intimidating!

Soft snow fell all night. The white farmhouses were a beautiful sight standing alone in enormous fields and meadows. This seemed strange to us, since in most of Europe, the farmers settled in small villages with the farmland circling the villages. The houses and the cities sparkled with bright lights. The whistle of the train was different from the trains in Europe, but at the same time, it was soothing. So we sat nestled near the warm window, looking at this new country. Our supper consisted of a sandwich, which all three of us shared. The problem was the language barrier. Even though we had a little money we did not know how to ask for food in English.

On the next morning, which was a Sunday, our train pulled into the station in Van Wert, Ohio. We were the only passengers to leave the train, but somehow we were motioned by the conductor, that this was our destination and it was really time to exit the train. In Germany any train station would be busy with a multitude of people, especially on the weekend. This one was totally deserted. Not a person was in sight. We were scared, but as soon as the train pulled away, to the relief of all three of us, we saw the smiling faces of my father's cousin, George Diener with his daughter, Alwine, and Forrest Williamson with his youngest daughter, Joan.

We rode in a new Lincoln to the Williamson farm, where we were greeted by the rest of the family and with a variety of food, which I had never before experienced. The German breakfasts are rather simple. This was a feast. The place and the family radiated with warmth and welcome, which was truly unique.

Through the thoughtfulness and kindness of the Williamson family, we lived in one of their farmhouses, which had been freshly painted and decorated. The house was filled with furniture and even the kitchen cupboards were full of food. For the first time since we left our homeland, I actually had not only my very own bed, but also my own bedroom, which was papered with pink roses and the windows were decorated with fluffy white curtains. Everything was very beautiful.

The Williamsons did not speak German and we could only visit with the Dieners on the weekends. We had to learn English quickly. Since I had to go to school the next morning, learning English was a priority. Every day I recorded as many new words as I could and in the evening my father and mother had an English lesson around our kitchen table. Through the mail we received papers that contained some English lessons through the government. We also studied diligently. I had the extra bonus of visiting with the Williamson daughters on weekends and many evenings when everyone went to bed Naomi, the mother, would teach me how to read in English. By Christmas we knew quite a lot of English.

So our adventure of assimilating to the American way of life began. Some events were humorous and enjoyable while others were sad and frustrating.

My two most memorable impressions of the American schools in the early fifties were red lipstick and bobby socks. Every morning in the coatroom at the local school the girls crowded around a large old mirror to adjust their lipstick and check out their appearance before the bell rang for the first period class. Of course, everyone wore white bobby socks and calf-length skirts. I was so impressed by how pretty those girls looked. I could hardly wait to have a tube of red lipstick of my own.

The next Christmas under the tree was a small package, which contained a shiny tube of red lipstick – thanks to the Williamsons. I was thrilled, but my parents were horrified at the thought of their young daughter going to school wearing lipstick. Wearing bobby socks in the middle of the winter was bad enough. Gradually they accepted the fact that we now lived in a different country. Besides, how could one be an American teenager without lipstick?

We missed our family and friends in Germany. At night when everything was quiet and I thought about my friends in Germany, I cried myself to sleep. I was fourteen now and a teenager, and it was very painful to be separated from every one back home. My mother was a real trooper, but to her "HOME" meant Crvenka.

Grandfather Stefan died that first Christmas. My aunt and uncle decided to stay in Germany. This devastated my mother.

The Williamson family was like an extended family. Because of their support and encouragement I developed a very positive attitude about life. On one specific occasion Naomi told my mother that I too could go to college some day. My mother was in shock, because she thought we were just poor refugees. Mother was wrong. In Germany we were refugees. Here we were becoming Americans and life was good. After completing high school, I graduated from college and later even graduate school, through the support of my parents. Life in America was good!

Eventually we moved to Mansfield, Ohio. We were closer to the German community and the work opportunity for my parents was better. They were over forty now and needed to have their own home. They both worked hard and were frugal with their money. Their accomplishments were great. Today they are buried in the Mansfield Cemetery in a section that marks the graves of many of their friends from their homeland.

America has blessed us in so many ways. Sometimes my thoughts wander back to our journey through World War II, our escape, and finally, coming to America. It was a miracle that all of us lived through those times. I thank God for his protection, Grandfather Stefan for his wisdom to escape and my father's foresight to bring us to America - a place where we enjoy many blessings and opportunities.

Meanwhile the rest of our family chose not to go through the regimentation to come to America. Willi and Elis, as young teenagers, had selected their plans for their careers and the thought of coming to a foreign country was too unsettling for them. As it turns out all three of my cousins have happy and successful lives in Germany.

Willi worked in the field of interior design and upholstery. Whenever I go to Germany and I hear about some of the projects he worked on, I am really impressed. Not only has he helped in the restoration and decoration of several castles in Bavaria, and fancy hotels in Munich, but also an apartment for the famous actress

Ingrid Bergman. He is married to Barbel, who is always a most gracious hostess, whenever we are there. Willi has one married son.

Elis worked in an office. Unfortunately she had much sorrow in her life. Not only did both of her babies die in infancy, but her husband Christian died in his early fifties. She has survived all these tragedies and lives alone in her beautiful house and enjoys the rest of her family and friends.

Baby Gretl amazingly survived and grew up into a very pretty young lady. She and her husband Karle are both fun-loving people. They have a married son and one grandson.

It has always been so very special to visit with them here in America or in Germany. They enjoy success and happiness and none of them can imagine living any place other than in Germany.

Both of my grandparents, my Aunt Lisi and my Uncle Wilhelm are buried in a family grave in a cemetery called Waldfriedhof, in Munich, Germany. Many of their friends and neighbors from Crvenka also have the graves beside them. A poem, written on a large white monument, honors all these people

who once called Crvenka their home.

Epilogue

eaving that turbulent October Sunday, 1944 was indeed a very wise decision. Those unfortunate citizens who stayed behind met torture, persecution and eventually death.

From October 8th through 13th everyone who wanted to leave had different opportunities to evacuate. Only a few days later, on October 18th, came the first Russian troops along with the Partisans, who brutally raped and killed people and began plundering and destroying the houses. Many other Russian troops also passed through Crvenka.

At the end of October the Serbian "Miliz" took control of the town. For a while there was a rivalry between the Tito-Communists and the Serbian-Loyalists to the monarchy, but the communists won. Consequently they issued a document, which was announced in our town square and stated the following rules:

All "Folksdeitscherei" (meaning Volksdeutsche; all national Germans), who did not actively support the national battle for freedom of their homeland and those who have fled, which included my family, have lost their Yugoslavian citizenship and the ownership and rights of inheritance to their property. In this manner 600,000 citizens who spoke German as their native language, lost their homeland, possessions, and protection under the law. Of course this announcement was just a façade. The people who stayed in there and were "loyal" to their homeland were persecuted immediately. They were chased out of their beds often in the middle of the night, driven like herds of animals into makeshift camps, and forced to work with very little food. It was a calculated plan to eliminate all ethnic Germans. Families were separated, men from women and children from their parents. They were grouped into camps according to their ability to work. Many old people, including a very dear aunt of my mother, found their death in Jarek. They were literally starved to death. The small children were separated and placed into camps like Kruschivle.

In December a group of young people from our town were deported to work in Russian coalmines, where most of them died.

Our Lutheran minister listed twelve such camps where our people from Crvenka were placed, but there were many more people from other towns in Yugoslavia who experienced the same fate.

The most serious of the above mentioned starvation camps were in Gakowa, Groß-Pisanitz, Jareck, and Kruschivle. The Donauschwaben received meager rations, if they were lucky, and always-cruel treatment. If the people of the Balkans needed workers, their camp director sold the Donauschwaben to them.

The stories of some of the survivors are documented in four volumes and are found in a museum to honor these people in Sindelfingen, Germany.

Beginning in December 1944 the Communist Partisan rule began which made a mockery of humanity and discarded every basic human right.

In January 1946 the communists openly recruited people to take over the towns and villages that were now empty. Several thousand came to Crvenka. They were given a house, a vineyard, livestock, cash, clothing, furniture, tools, food, a radio, and other equipment. Of course these were all taken from the Donauschwaben.

There was a constant coming and going of the new people. The houses were looted and many destroyed. Later we found out that all the front windows in our house were destroyed, which my parents had built only two years earlier. The looters were playing target practice with jars of my mother's canned fruit.

In the end 86,000 people lost their lives. We too would have been numbered in these statistics, if the Communists had not denied us entrance into our town. Unlike our train, many others were permitted to enter and went home, only to find death in a starvation camp.

Not until many years later did all these events come together. Only then did we realize how fortunate we were. When we left on that fateful Sunday in October 1944, we were only ten days away from the Russian take over. After the war was over and we wanted to return home, our train was only fifteen minutes away from our home. Each time we were spared. Without God's intervention, certainly we all would have perished.

And so ends a chapter in the history of a group of human beings, the Donauschwaben, whose only crime was having a German heritage. Crvenka regressed in culture, civilization, economics and Christianity. All of the churches were destroyed along with other public buildings.

The inhumanity against humanity is incomprehensible, and yet this is only a very small part of all the events that took place during this horrible war.

In spite of all the hardships, the human spirit has a powerful resiliency that rises above many adversities. So it was with the Donauschwaben. These people were scattered all over the globe, but have found new lives, built new homes and been blessed with overall success.

Batschka Song

Precious Batschka, beloved homeland!

How far, how far, are you away?

The earth's most beautiful lowland,

Gladly I give my life for you!

Beloved homeland, golden ground,

I will always give you praise unbound.

When death will take my sight,

You will always still be my light!

And in the evening as the sun sets in the sky,

I will bow in prayer my knee,

So enormous is my pain for thee,

Because my heart aches for thee.

Weeping could I, forever weeping,

Over all that I have seen.

From the homeland all are fleeing.

Peace they will never find again.

As the autumn rains are falling

On their trembling, freezing bodies,

And softly I hear children weeping.

Lord God, Almighty, how can this be?

One hundred fifty years we labored

Till those fields in splendor stood.

Then the storm of time away us swept,

Like autumn leaves into a net.

Like little sheep, lost in the meadows,

We follow along endless highways.

We halt in rows of columns.

Where we will go, no one knows.

As our precious homeland vanished,

Horror is what I have found.

In your honor I raise my hand,

And whisper: Farewell my sweet Batschkaland!

Heinrich Peter   8/10/1944

Translated by Anne Holden   Fall 1999

Die Batschka

Heimat deutscher Protestanten in Partnerschaft mit anderen Konfessionen und anderen Völkern

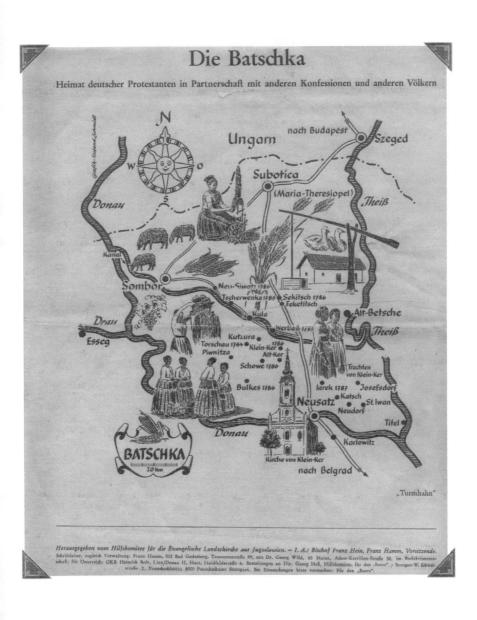

„Turmhahn"

Herausgegeben vom Hilfskomitee für die Evangelische Landeskirche aus Jugoslawien. – I. A.: Bischof Franz Hein, Franz Hamm, Vorsitzende.
Schriftleiter, zugleich Verwaltung: Franz Hamm, 532 Bad Godesberg, Teutonenstraße 99, mit Dr. Georg Wild, 65 Mainz, Adam-Karrillon-Straße 50, im Redaktionsausschuß; für Österreich: OKR Heinrich Rohr, Linz/Donau II, Hart, Heidfeldstraße 6. Bestellungen an Dir. Georg Heß, Hilfskomitee, für den „Boten", ; Stuttgart-W, Schwabstraße. 1. Postscheckkonto 9005 Postscheckamt Stuttgart. Bei Einsendungen bitte vermerken: Für den „Boten".

Heinrich (Henry) Jung 1906–1977

Katarina (Käthe) Stefan Jung 1909–1988

This is the ancestral family home at Frankelbach, Pfalz of the Jung family.

Their house belonged to the grandfather of Anne's ancestor
Michael Johann Jung who left his home in Germany and
began a new life in Crvenka, Batschka, Yugoslavia in 1775.
The following words were written above the front door in German.

This house stands in God's hand

May he keep it safe from fire and want.

Photo of Anne's father's family
From left to right: Wilhelm (William) Jakob, with Heinrich
(Henry, Anne's father)
Katharina, Jakob and Katharina Dautermann Jung.

Photo of Anne's
mother's family

From left to right: Paul Stefan,
Lisi and Katy.
In the back, Elisabeth (Diener)
Stefan.

Anne at age one and one half years with her parents.
Taken in the spring of 1938

Anne's Grandmother
Grandmother Goetz at the age of 45. Taken in 1925.

Kindergarten friends, Elis (Anne's cousin) Leni, Inge and Anne

Anne wearing her grand white dress made out of two different fabrics,
with the three red glass buttons.
She is standing next to her cousin Willi,
Elis and Gretl. Taken in the summer of 1947

*Anne's Aunt Lisi and
Uncle Wilhelm with
Willi, Gretl and Elis*

Summer of 1947 at the Zoo.

Children from the Implerlager, a refugee camp in Munich.

All of these children were from Crvenka.

Left to right: Anne, friends Elis and Gretl, sixth to the right. Almost all of these cloth *came from American packages.*

The little boy in white, front left, is Paul. His sister, fourth from front left, Alwin *re the children of George and Christine Diener, Anne's father's second cousin, wh* *helped us to come to America.*

Summer of 1948

*Elis and Anne. Anne and her cousin are standing in front
of their school, Götzinger Volksschule*

Winter of 1951

Spring of 1951
Anne's grandparents Stefan with their grandchildren from left
to right. Anne, Grandfather Stefan, Gretl, Grandmother, Elis
and Willi in back

October 1951 Shortly before Anne left Germany.
These were her best friends.

Anne's sponsors, Forrest and Naomi Williamson with their
daughters, Joan, Lois, Alice and Leaha. 1953

Anne's high school graduation picture 1956

College days.

*Anne and her fiancée, Ron Holden at Sweetheart formal
at Wittenberg University 1957*

College days.

Spring formal at Wittenberg University. 1958

Anne's wedding day.

September 13, 1958. Ron and Anne Holden Mansfield, Ohio.

Our trip to Germany 1963.

Left to right Ron Holden, Anne, Aunt Lisi and Uncle Wilhelm. In the back author's mother, Käthe, Gretl with Anne's daughter, Anita.

Anne's family, children and grandchildren. Thanksgiving 2001

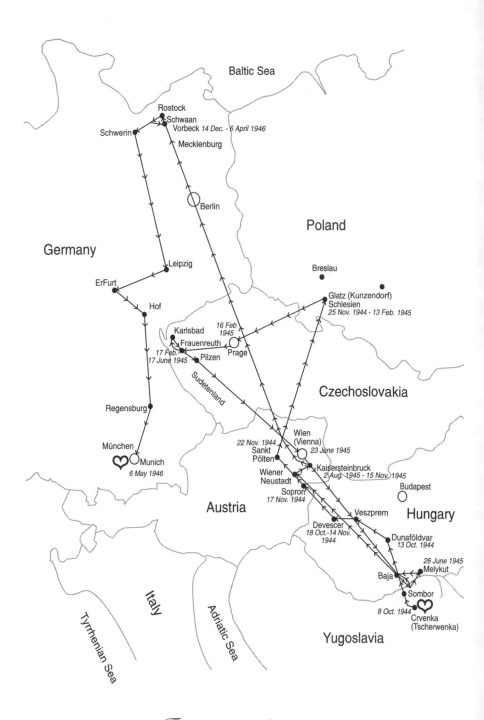

This is a map of the escape.